The Heroes Handbook

for Living Life as a Spiritual Adventure

Kenneth David Lee

Table of contents

I would like to dedicate this book to my wife, Lauren. You inspire me to be my favorite version of myself.

And to my parents, for their ever-present love and support. I am your creation.

Lastly, to my boys: Speak the truth, defend the helpless, uphold the weak, let your heart know only virtue, and may your wrath undo the wicked.

Introduction

I n the pages of this book lies a mystery that goes beyond tradition, beyond doctrine, and reaches into the very core of human longing. It's a secret that resonates with something deep within us all—a universal cry that echoes with the profound desire to be part of something bigger, something grander.

The story of Jesus is not just a tale of divine intervention. It's a narrative that connects with the foundational yearning we all share: to be a hero. Yes, you read that right. You are that hero. Your life, your story, has the potential to change the world. Maybe not the whole world, but certainly the world of those around you. Those you love, those you meet, those you serve.

This book is more than words on a page; it's a tool in the hands of a God who knows you and loves you. It's a guide that will help you understand your own heroic tale, one where Jesus has already walked the path before you and now waits to be your companion along the way.

We'll journey together through the well-known steps of the Hero's Journey, or the monomyth as made famous by Joseph

Campbell. We'll explore the stages, the trials, and the triumphs. And along the way, my prayer is that you will begin to see yourself in the process, recognizing that you are not just another face in the crowd.

You are special. You are chosen. You are the one for whom God sent His Son.

The adventure awaits. The path is before you. The question is, are you ready to step into your story and embrace the hero that you were meant to be? The stakes are high, the journey is challenging, but the rewards are eternal.

Let's embark on this adventure together, and discover the incredible purpose and destiny that await you.

Welcome to your heroic journey. Welcome to the mystery, the challenge, the transformation. Welcome to a story that has been waiting for you since the beginning of time.

One

The Divine Whisper

Have you ever felt a nudge, a subtle prompting that seemed to guide you towards something greater? It's like a whisper in your ear, a pull in your heart that calls you towards something beyond yourself. You can't shake it off; you can't ignore it. It's a soft voice, almost drowned out by the noises of daily life, but it persists, gentle and unrelenting.

Imagine standing at a crossroads, unsure which path to take. You look down one road, then another, each stretching into the unknown. And just when you feel most lost, you hear it - that whisper. It doesn't shout, it doesn't demand, but it guides. It's a sense that the path you're meant to walk has been there all along, waiting for you to take the first step.

I remember standing at the shore of the Sea of Galilee, staring at the calm, glass-like surface, and feeling that same whisper. I could almost hear the gentle lap of waves, the distant laughter of fishermen, the murmur of Jesus's voice as He taught from a simple boat.

The place where Jesus once walked, taught, healed, and lived seemed to hum with a divine frequency. It was alive, pulsating with a rhythm that reached deep into my soul. It was the epicenter of a story that transcended time, a story that, believe it or not, has everything to do with you and me.

Standing there, with my feet in the very sand where He may have stood, I couldn't help but feel connected to something far greater than myself. The lessons taught on that shore weren't confined to history or trapped in ancient scrolls. They were alive, echoing across the centuries, calling to anyone who would listen.

That whisper, that pull, is not just a fleeting emotion or a mere coincidence. It's a calling. A calling to explore, to understand, to grow. It's an invitation to step into a story that has the power to transform lives.

It's easy to dismiss such moments as mere feelings or wishful thinking. But what if that whisper is something more? What if it's a voice calling you towards a purpose and identity that's been there all along, waiting for you to discover?

The Sea of Galilee might be miles away, but the whisper is as close as your heartbeat. It's a story that reaches across the ages, a journey that begins with a single step, a calling that's as personal as it is universal.

And it's a calling that starts with a whisper.

But let's rewind the tape for a moment and start at the beginning.

More than two millennia ago, in a small town called Bethlehem, the world was introduced to a child who would grow up to change everything. His birth wasn't heralded by celebrity magazines or trending hashtags but by stars, angels, and prophecies. It was a moment etched into the very fabric of history, filled with mystery, wonder, and divine purpose.

Picture this: a young woman, a simple carpenter, and a journey to an overcrowded town. There's no room at the inn, no lavish banquet, no press coverage. Instead, a humble stable becomes the birthplace of a King.

The night sky lights up, not with fireworks, but with a star so bright that it guides wise men from distant lands. Shepherds, the lowest of the low in society, are the first to hear the news, not from town criers but from angels singing in the night.

Why Jesus? What made this carpenter's son from Nazareth the embodiment of a hero's journey unlike any other? Why not a prince, a warrior, or a scholar? Why a child born in a stable, in a town that most had overlooked?

This is where the story of Jesus defies all our expectations. His journey wasn't about prestige, power, or earthly glory. It was about humility, love, and a connection to the very heart of humanity. It's about God reaching down, not in thunderous might but in gentle compassion.

Jesus's life started in obscurity but led to a path that would shake the very foundations of the world. He didn't conquer nations; He conquered hearts. He didn't lead armies; He led souls towards redemption.

And what could His story possibly have to do with our lives today? It's a question that resonates, isn't it? How can a tale so ancient, so distant, have any bearing on our modern, fast-paced lives?

The answer lies not in the grandeur of miracles or the complexity of theological debates but in the simplicity of His message. A message of love, forgiveness, service, and grace. A message that transcends time and speaks to the very core of what it means to be human.

You see, the story of Jesus is not confined to dusty pages or historical artifacts. It's alive, vibrant, and deeply personal. It's a story that invites us into a journey of discovery, a path that leads to understanding not only the divine but ourselves.

So let's take that journey. Let's explore the life of a carpenter's son who became the Savior of the world. Let's discover how His story is our story, His path our path, His love our love.

In the end, we may find that the story of Jesus is not just about history or religion; it's about life itself. It's a story that connects us to the very essence of what it means to be human. It's a story about answering a call, embracing a mission, and embarking on a journey that defines the very core of our existence.

Consider for a moment what it means to truly live. Not just to exist, but to thrive, to resonate with a sense of purpose that goes beyond our daily routines. Think about those moments when you feel most alive, most connected to something greater. That, my friend, is what the story of Jesus touches on. It's about finding our true north, our reason for being.

It's about more than dogma, rules, or rituals. It's about love, compassion, forgiveness, and selflessness. It's about viewing life not as a solitary quest but as a shared journey, where we are all connected by a common thread of humanity.

The story of Jesus starts not with a loud proclamation but with a whisper, a divine calling that reaches across time and space. It's subtle, like the soft rustle of leaves in the wind or the gentle touch of a loved one's hand. It's a voice that doesn't shout or demand but invites, guides, and encourages.

You may have heard this whisper in a moment of quiet reflection or during a time of desperate need. It's a voice that calls us towards something higher, something noble, something profoundly good. It's a voice that transcends barriers and breaks down walls, connecting us to a timeless truth that speaks to the very soul of who we are.

And, as we'll discover, it's a calling that invites us to join in on a journey that promises not only to reveal who Jesus really is but who we are meant to be. It's not a journey of self-aggrandizement or earthly success but a journey towards authenticity, empathy, and divine love.

It's a path that challenges us to step out of our comfort zones, to question our assumptions, to embrace those around us with a love that is unconditional and all-encompassing. It's a path that doesn't promise ease or comfort but offers fulfillment, joy, and a sense of belonging that no earthly treasure can match.

Are you ready to hear that whisper? Are you prepared to take that step, to embrace that calling, to embark on a journey that may very well change your life?

For in the story of a carpenter's son from Nazareth, we find a roadmap to our true selves. In His words, His actions, His love, we find a guide to what it truly means to be human.

The Pathway

Imagine, if you will, standing at the trailhead of a path untraveled. It winds through valleys and mountains, across rivers and deserts. At times, it seems daunting, filled with uncertainty and challenges. But it's also beckoning, alive with possibility and promise.

This is not a journey for the faint-hearted, nor is it a path of least resistance. It's a pilgrimage, a sacred adventure that calls us to step out of the familiar and into the unknown. It's a journey that asks us to let go of preconceived notions, to open our hearts, and to embrace a story that has resonated with millions for over two millennia.

But why walk this path? Why follow in the footsteps of a carpenter's son from a time so distant?

Because, as we'll find, the life of Jesus is not merely a historical account or a moral guidebook. It's a living narrative, one that intersects with our own lives in ways we might never have imagined. It's a story that speaks to our deepest desires, our greatest fears, our most profound questions.

As we explore the teachings, the miracles, the moments of grace and truth in Jesus's life, we might just discover echoes of our own story. We might hear that divine whisper not as a distant sound but as a voice speaking directly to us, guiding us towards a purpose that is uniquely ours.

And in uncovering that purpose, in embracing that identity, we find something extraordinary. We find a way to live that goes beyond mere existence, beyond the chase for success or the pursuit of happiness. We find a way to live that is anchored in love, grounded in faith, and filled with a joy that transcends all circumstances.

We find a way to be truly human.

So yes, grab those walking shoes. Pack a bag filled with curiosity, hope, and a willingness to explore. Leave behind the baggage of doubt, fear, and prejudice. And let's walk this path together.

Let's explore the life of Jesus, not as distant observers but as fellow travelers. Let's hear the divine whisper not as a relic of the past but as a call to action in the present. Let's uncover the purpose and identity that lie waiting for each of us, hidden not in the pages of a book but in the depths of our hearts.

For this journey is not just about understanding a figure from history; it's about discovering who we are, why we're here, and how we can live a life that truly matters.

The path is before us, the call is clear, and the adventure awaits. Shall we begin?

Two

Crossing the Threshold

We all stand at a threshold at some point in our lives. You know the moment I'm talking about. It's that heart-pounding, pulse-racing, soul-stirring moment when you find yourself on the edge of something big, something significant, something life-changing.

It's that line between the familiar and the unknown. On one side, there's comfort, safety, predictability. It's the world as you know it, the life you've always lived. It's your normal.

But then, on the other side, there's something else, something that tugs at your heart, something that whispers to your soul. It's the unknown, the adventurous, the extraordinary. It's a calling, a dream, a destiny. It's your future.

This threshold is not just a physical place; it's a spiritual space. It's a choice, a decision that holds within it the very essence of our life's purpose and destiny. It's a doorway to a new beginning, a gateway to a new journey, a portal to a new life.

Remember Sam Gamgee from "The Lord of the Rings"? There he was, on the edge of the Shire, venturing farther than he had ever been. "If I take one more step, it'll be the farthest away from home I've ever been." It was more than just a geographical boundary; it was a psychological barrier, an emotional hurdle, a spiritual frontier.

And then there was Jesus, at the Jordan River, about to be baptized, about to begin His ministry, about to step into His destiny. It wasn't just a religious ritual; it was a divine moment, a cosmic threshold, a holy adventure.

And here's the thing: We all face these thresholds. Maybe it's a new job, a new relationship, a new challenge. Maybe it's a new understanding, a new perspective, a new direction. Maybe it's a new you.

The question is, will you cross it? Will you take the step? Will you embrace the adventure? Will you seize the destiny? Will you live the life?

It won't be easy. Thresholds can be scary, intimidating, daunting. But they can also be exciting, exhilarating, empowering.

So, take a deep breath. Take a good look. Take a bold step. For in crossing the threshold, you're not just changing your location; you're transforming your life.

And remember, you're not alone. You have a Guide, a Companion, a Friend in Jesus. He knows the way. He's been there before. He's with you now.

Jesus at the Threshold

I want you to picture the Jordan River. The sun is glinting off the water. There's a crowd gathered on the banks, murmuring in anticipation. There's John the Baptist, wild-eyed, passionate, immersed in his mission. And there, stepping to the water's edge, is Jesus.

It's a threshold moment.

His feet are still on dry land, but He's about to wade into the current. It's a literal and symbolic line between His past life and His divine mission. As He stands there, ready to be baptized, there's a choice in front of Him. It's a choice to leave behind the carpenter's shop, to step out of the shadows of Nazareth, to embark on a journey that would forever change the world.

Imagine that moment. The water's edge. The expectant crowd. The knowing look in John the Baptist's eyes. Can you see it? Can you feel it? This is not just a moment in history; it's a moment in eternity.

Jesus knew what was at stake. He knew that crossing this threshold meant stepping into His calling, embracing His destiny, fulfilling His purpose. He knew it wouldn't be easy. He knew it would demand everything of Him. It would mean facing rejection, embracing suffering, defying expectations, confronting evil. It would mean the cross. Yet, He chose to step.

Why?

Because He understood something profound. He understood that the threshold is not just about leaving something behind; it's about stepping into something more. It's about embracing the adventure, the mission, the purpose that gives life its meaning and its essence.

He knew that the Jordan River was not just a place of baptism; it was a gateway to destiny. He knew that the water was not just a symbol of cleansing; it was a sign of commitment. He knew that the step was not just a physical act; it was a spiritual pledge.

He knew that the threshold was not just a transition; it was a transformation. It was a turning point, a tipping point, a point of no return.

Your Threshold

So, what about you? Where's your threshold? What's your Shire that you need to leave behind? What's your Jordan River that you need to cross? What's your adventure, your mission, your purpose that's calling you forth?

Here's the truth: We all face these moments. We all stand at these lines. We all hear these calls. The question is, will we step? Will we cross? Will we embrace the adventure that awaits?

Remember, it's almost guaranteed that you won't come back the same way you left. And that's the beauty of it. For in the stepping, in the crossing, in the embracing, we find ourselves, our true selves, our best selves.

A Dangerous Yet Rewarding Journey

But let me be clear. This isn't about a casual stroll down a well-trodden path. Following Jesus is an adventure, and like all true adventures, it comes with its share of dangers and challenges. When you make the decision to follow the ultimate hero, you are not merely signing up for comfort and ease; you are enlisting in a mission that will lead you into battles that may at times feel overwhelming.

This is not a journey for the faint of heart. Jesus Himself warned that to follow Him would mean taking up a cross, facing opposition, confronting our deepest fears and insecurities. It means standing up for justice, loving unconditionally, and sacrificing self for the greater good. It's about going to places you've never been, doing things you've never done, and becoming someone you've never been.

And yet, here's the beautiful paradox: In the very challenges and struggles of this journey, we find our true strength, our true joy, and our true purpose. The battles are not for our defeat but for our growth, our refinement, our transformation. They are designed for our good!

The Call to Follow

So, here's the invitation. It's more than a casual suggestion; it's a heartfelt plea, a soul-stirring call to action. Will you follow Jesus? Will you embark on this incredible journey? Will you embrace the adventure that is life with Him?

You don't have to have it all figured out. You don't have to be perfect. You don't even have to know what the next step looks like. All you need is a willing heart, an open mind, and a readiness to act.

If that's you, then simply say "yes." Yes to Jesus. Yes to the journey. Yes to the adventure. Yes to life in all its fullness and all its beauty.

Start where you are. Take a moment to reflect, to pray, to open your heart. Speak to Jesus like you would to a friend. Invite Him into your life. Ask Him to guide you, to strengthen you, to fill you with His love and His peace.

Remember, this isn't about religion; it's about relationship. It's about connecting with the one who created you, loves you, and has an extraordinary plan for your life.

So, what do you say? Are you ready to cross that threshold? Are you ready to step into the unknown, to embrace the dangers, to conquer the challenges, to live the adventure?

Jesus is waiting, arms open, smile wide, heart ready. All He needs is your "yes." All He wants is you.

Welcome to the journey of a lifetime. Welcome to the adventure of following Jesus. It's the best decision you'll ever make, and it starts right here, right now, with you.

Three

The Threshold Guardian

Y ou know, there's a dark figure lurking around. Not hiding in the shadows as you might expect, but weaving itself right into our everyday lives. This enemy, whose existence has been debated and argued about for centuries, might seem like a myth or a metaphor to some. But the Bible leaves no room for ambiguity. It names this entity, calling it Satan, the Father of Lies.

Once upon a time, this being was a messenger, an angel of all things. Can you believe that? An angel. A creature of light, given the sacred task of conveying God's love, light, goodness, and glory. But what did he choose to bring instead? Lies, death, despair, trickery. His desire, his insatiable thirst, is to steal, kill, and destroy you with lies.

But Satan's tactics are even more sinister than that. He doesn't just lie to you. He wants you to believe the lies so much that you live them out. Those intrusive thoughts, those whispers of self-doubt, and insecurity become part of your reality. You start to see yourself not as God sees you but through a distorted lens.

Why? Because "satan" means "accuser." And that's what he wants to do—accuse you, make you feel guilty, unworthy, defeated. But why the obsession with accusing us? Why the relentless pursuit to bring us down?

It's fear. Satan is afraid of you and me. Afraid of us taking our rightful place as the chosen children of a great God. Afraid of us walking out God's goodness every single day, living lives filled with promise, love, and joy that transform the world around us.

Satan's goal is to make us bitter, gnarly, hateful. He wants us to bring that hell to others. He wants to take the heavenly mission we've been given and twist it into something ugly and destructive.

But here's the thing: we don't have to fall for it. We have a guide, a protector, a loving Father who has given us the tools to recognize the lies and to stand strong. We have the truth, the Word, and the community of believers to support us.

You're a Wizard, Harry

Picture Harry Potter, the boy with the lightning-shaped scar, who grew up believing he was just an unfortunate orphan, doomed to a life of misery with the Dursleys. The Dursleys, in their greed, ignorance, and fear of the unknown, wanted to make him forget who he was, the magical lineage from which he came. They lied to him, mistreated him, and locked away the truth of his destiny, all to maintain their control over him.

Harry's life under the Dursleys' roof was filled with trials and tribulations. From sleeping in a cupboard under the stairs to wearing Dudley's hand-me-downs, from being excluded and demeaned to having his true identity hidden, the lies weighed on him, keeping him from the world where he truly belonged.

But what if Harry had never learned the truth? What if he never got on that bike with Hagrid? Imagine a life where the Dursleys' lies remained unbroken, where Harry never stepped onto the Hogwarts Express, never met Ron and Hermione, never learned to wave a wand.

It would have been a tragedy, a story of potential wasted, a magical destiny unfulfilled. Harry would have continued to live a life of dull monotony, never knowing what he was capable of, never discovering the incredible world that awaited him.

Harry's story isn't all that different from ours. The Liar himself, Satan, wants us to forget in whose image we were made, and the tremendous power that we hold. Just like the Dursleys with Harry, Satan wants to keep us confined, ignorant of our true identity and potential. He wants us to ignore the spark of divinity within us, the heavenly calling we have.

But unlike Harry, our true calling is not a secret. Our lineage is not hidden in dusty letters or concealed by deceitful relatives. Our God reaches out to us with love, calling us to a life of adventure, a life of purpose.

A Beautiful Truth

Here's the good news. Jesus came to cut through the noise, the lies, the static that fills our minds with doubt and fear. He came to tell us that we are all His children, that the life of adventure is ours for the taking. He assures us that we can rise above the petty systems of this world and join Him in heavenly places, where love reigns supreme and where our true selves can shine.

I've sat with many who tell me of the thoughts of unworthiness that cross their minds. They've shared the intrusive thoughts that keep pulling them down, like anchors tied to their souls. These thoughts are relentless, and they whisper a narrative of failure, of disappointment, of insignificance.

But let me tell you something: This is not a voice of hope, and it is definitely not God's voice. I think one of the worst things evangelical Christianity ever did was give people the voice of self-criticism and called it God. This voice that tells you that you're never good enough, that you're constantly failing, that you should be ashamed. That's not the voice of a loving Father. That's the voice of an accuser, an enemy.

God is not against you; He is for you. He's not sitting in judgment, waiting for you to slip up; He's in your corner, cheering you on. He's not mad at you; He's mad about you! He sees your potential, your worth, your unique place in His grand story.

So my friends, today I want you to recognize the lies for what they are. When you hear that voice telling you that you're unworthy, that you don't matter, that you're a failure, recognize it. Label it. Call it out as a lie. Because Jesus says you are worth it, again and again.

Don't let the enemy of your soul define who you are or what you're capable of. You were created in the image of God, destined for great things. You have a role in this grand story, a purpose that goes beyond your wildest dreams. Embrace that truth, and let it propel you forward into the life of adventure, joy, and fulfillment that God has prepared for you. You are not just a character in someone else's tale; you are the hero of your own story, a story of redemption, transformation, and victory.

Besting the Guardians

So how do we fight this enemy? How do we stand against the lies that aim to pull us down and derail us from our destiny? It's a battle that requires more than mere determination. It needs a strategy grounded in faith, truth, and community. Here's what that might look like:

Know Your Identity in Christ: Remember who you are. You're not just a face in the crowd or a nameless entity drifting through life. You're a child of God, loved, cherished, and created with purpose. Hold onto this identity, let it anchor you in times of doubt, and allow it to be the foundation of everything you do.

Stay Connected to the Truth: The Bible isn't just a book; it's a lifeline. Dive into the Word, let it guide you, strengthen you, and remind you of God's promises. When the lies creep in, reach for Scripture. Let it be your weapon against deception, a sword that cuts through confusion, a lamp that lights your path.

Embrace Community: We were never meant to walk this journey alone. Surround yourself with people who will affirm you, encourage you, and remind you of the truth. Find friends, mentors, and fellow believers who won't just nod in agreement but will challenge you, pray for you, and stand with you in the battle against lies.

Listen to Jesus: Tune out the lies and tune into His voice. In prayer, in silence, in worship, let Him tell you how much you mean to Him. Let Him remind you of your worth, your calling, your place in His heart. This isn't just positive thinking; it's aligning yourself with the voice of love, hope, and truth.

The adventure with Jesus is yours for the taking. But to embark on this grand journey, we must first defeat the lies that seek to hold us back. It won't be easy. It will require vigilance, perseverance, and courage. But you've got what it takes. You have the tools, the allies, the guidance. Now, it's time to rise above and claim your victory.

Remember, the enemy may be relentless, but he has already been defeated. Your victory is not a distant dream but a present reality, anchored in Christ's love for you. So stand firm, march forward, and let your life be a testament to the power of truth over deception, of love over fear, of faith over doubt.

Four

The Guide, Mentor, and Helper

Every hero needs a guide. Think about it. In those great stories, those timeless tales, those epic adventures, there's always a wise mentor, a faithful guide, a dependable friend who helps the hero navigate the unknown. This figure isn't just a side character; they're essential. They're the ones who provide wisdom, encouragement, and guidance at critical moments. They often see something in the hero that the hero doesn't see in themselves.

Consider Obi-Wan Kenobi in 'Star Wars.' His mentorship of Luke Skywalker wasn't merely about training him in the ways of the Jedi; it was about awakening something within Luke, something profound, something powerful. Obi-Wan knew that Luke was more than just a farm boy from Tatooine; he was the hope of the galaxy.

Or think about Dumbledore in 'Harry Potter.' His relationship with Harry wasn't just about teaching spells and potions; it was about nurturing Harry's courage, integrity, and leadership. Dumbledore's wisdom guided Harry through trials and challenges, helping him discover not just his magical abilities but his moral compass.

And don't forget Gandalf from 'The Lord of the Rings.' His guidance of Frodo wasn't just about a perilous journey to Mount Doom; it was about a transformational journey of character, resilience, and purpose. Gandalf's insight and encouragement helped Frodo grow from a timid hobbit into a heroic figure who could change the course of history.

These mentors, these guides, these friends play a pivotal role in the hero's journey. They don't do the hero's work for them, but they make the work possible. They don't walk the path for the hero, but they light the way. They don't take away the hero's struggles, but they help the hero make sense of them.

In our own lives, we have our own guides and mentors. Maybe they're a parent, a teacher, a friend, or a spiritual leader. Whoever they are, they're there to help us navigate our own epic adventures, our own unique journeys.

But perhaps the greatest mentor, the ultimate guide, the most faithful friend we can have on our journey is the Holy Spirit. Just as these fictional guides led their heroes, the Holy Spirit is here to lead us. Just as these mentors saw something extraordinary in their heroes, the Holy Spirit sees something extraordinary in us. Just as these wise figures were pivotal to the story, the Holy Spirit is pivotal to our story.

Jesus and the Holy Spirit

From the moment of His baptism, Jesus was led by the Holy Spirit. The scriptures tell us that after His baptism, the Spirit led Jesus into the wilderness, where He was tested and tried (Matthew 4:1). But this was not a solitary event. Throughout His ministry, Jesus was in constant communion with the Holy Spirit, leaning into His guidance, following His promptings, depending on His wisdom.

Consider the profound words of Jesus Himself: 'I do nothing on my own but speak just what the Father has taught me' (John 8:28). This statement wasn't a metaphor or an exaggeration; it was a declaration of dependence. Jesus was expressing that His actions, His words, His very life were in complete alignment with the will of the Father, guided by the Holy Spirit. It was a relationship of perfect trust and perfect obedience.

Jesus's relationship with the Holy Spirit was not casual or occasional; it was vital and intentional. It was the source of His strength, the fountain of His wisdom, the anchor of His mission. Time and again, when faced with a difficult decision or situation, Jesus would retreat to spend time in prayer, communing with the Holy Spirit. Before choosing His twelve disciples (Luke 6:12-13), before facing the agonizing reality of the cross (Matthew 26:36-44), Jesus withdrew to seek the guidance, the comfort, the empowerment of the Holy Spirit.

These weren't mere rituals or religious exercises; these were sacred moments, intimate encounters, transformative experiences. In the solitude of the wilderness, on the mountaintops of prayer, in the quiet of the night, Jesus found not just answers but alignment, not just solutions but surrender, not just direction but destiny.

What's the lesson for us? If Jesus, the Son of God, relied on the Holy Spirit, how much more should we? If Jesus, the Savior of the world, needed time with the Holy Spirit, how much more do we?

Our relationship with the Holy Spirit shouldn't be a side note to our faith; it should be the center of our faith. It shouldn't be an occasional practice; it should be a daily priority. It shouldn't be a religious ritual; it should be a relational reality.

Our Guide, Mentor, and Helper

So, what about us? If Jesus, the Son of God, the Savior of the world, needed the Holy Spirit as His guide, how much more do we? Think about it for a moment. Consider the implications. Contemplate the possibilities.

The good news is that the same Holy Spirit who guided Jesus is here to guide us. The same Holy Spirit who mentored Jesus is here to mentor us. The same Holy Spirit who helped Jesus is here to help us. Yes, the Holy Spirit, the Comforter that Jesus promised in Acts 1:8, is available to each one of us, ready to inform, guide, and launch us into our destiny.

This is not a distant relationship; it's an intimate one. It's not a formal connection; it's a personal one. It's not a theoretical concept; it's a practical reality. The Holy Spirit is not an abstract idea; He's an active presence. He's not an impersonal force; He's a personal friend.

Do you remember the scene in 'Star Wars: A New Hope' when Luke is making his final run on the Death Star? The moment is critical, the stakes are high, the tension is palpable. And there, in the midst of it all, Luke hears the voice of Obi-Wan, his wise mentor, gently guiding him: 'Use the Force, Luke.' At that moment, Luke turns off his imperfect instruments and trusts the voice, trusts the wisdom, trusts the Force. And he succeeds.

That's a powerful image, isn't it? But it's more than just a fictional scene; it's a spiritual truth. It's a picture of how the Holy Spirit works in our lives. Whenever we are feeling lost, whenever we don't know which way to turn, whenever we are afraid of the road ahead, the Comforter comes in. The Holy Spirit speaks to us, reassures us, guides us, empowers us. He reminds us that everything we need to succeed is already in us, through Him.

So, here's the invitation: Let's open our hearts to the Holy Spirit. Let's tune our ears to His voice. Let's follow His guidance. Let's lean into His wisdom. Let's embrace His comfort. Let's live our lives not by our limited understanding but by His limitless power.

How to Lean into the Holy Spirit

How do we lean into the Holy Spirit as our guide, mentor, and helper? It's a profound question, a practical question, a personal question.

Awareness: It starts with awareness, with recognizing that the Holy Spirit is not just an abstract idea but a living presence. He's real. He's active. He's here. And He wants to be involved in your life, in your thoughts, in your decisions, in your struggles, in your victories.

Openness: It continues with openness, with inviting the Holy Spirit into our daily lives, our everyday decisions, our constant challenges. This is not a one-time invitation; it's an ongoing one. It's not a Sunday morning request; it's a Monday through Sunday commitment. Open your heart. Open your mind. Open your life.

Obedience: It deepens with obedience, with listening to the Holy Spirit's promptings, following His guidance, depending on His wisdom. This is where the rubber meets the road. This is where faith becomes action. This is where belief becomes behavior. Obey His voice, even when it's a whisper. Follow His lead, even when it's a nudge. Trust His wisdom, even when it's a mystery.

Understanding: The Holy Spirit helps us understand the nature of our loving Heavenly Father. He reveals the heart of God, the love of God, the grace of God. He helps us grasp deep spiritual truths that transform our thoughts, our beliefs, our lives. Like the verse in Romans 12:2 that says that we will be transformed by the renewing of our minds. That's the work of the Holy Spirit. That's the power of the Holy Spirit.

Growth: With the Holy Spirit as our guide, we grow in wisdom and understanding. We dig into the Scriptures, and they come alive. We read the words, and they speak to us. We ponder the truths, and they change us. We delve into the mysteries, and they unfold before us. It's a journey of discovery, a journey of growth, a journey of transformation.

So here's the challenge: Lean into the Holy Spirit. Become aware of His presence. Open your life to His guidance. Obey His promptings. Understand His revelations. Grow in His wisdom.

You Were Created for This

Imagine your life, your journey, with the Holy Spirit as your guide, mentor, and helper. Let your mind wander into this profound truth. Picture the confidence, the courage, the clarity that comes from knowing that you're not alone, that you're guided by the same Spirit who guided Jesus.

Confidence: Confidence comes from knowing that the Spirit of God, the same Spirit that hovered over the waters at creation, resides in you. It's not a fleeting feeling; it's a solid certainty. It's a deep-rooted assurance that no matter what comes your way, you have the Creator's Spirit within you. Unlike the mythical mentors, He will never leave you.

Courage: Courage blossoms when you know you are walking hand in hand with the Holy Spirit. It's the strength to face the unknown, the resolve to overcome obstacles, the bravery to stand for what's right. It's the courage that enables you to step out in faith, even when the world tells you to retreat in fear.

Clarity: Clarity shines when the fog of confusion lifts, and the Holy Spirit illuminates the path. It's the understanding that comes when you listen to His whisper, follow His lead, trust His guidance. It's the vision that transcends human sight and perceives divine insight.

But here's the stunning realization: This is not a new idea; it's an ancient design. It's not a modern concept; it's a timeless truth. You see, we were created with this in mind, all the way from the Garden of Eden, where Adam and Eve walked with God in the 'cool of the day.' That 'cool of the day' is the Hebrew word 'Ruach,' which means breath of God, and it is also used for the Spirit of God. We were meant to be Spirit Walkers, always in communion with the Father's Spirit.

Imagine that! You were designed to walk with the Spirit of God, to talk with the Spirit of God, to live with the Spirit of God. You were fashioned to be in constant fellowship, in delightful dialogue, in wonderful communion.

This is not a distant dream; it's a daily reality. This is not a lofty ideal; it's a loving invitation. This is not a theoretical concept; it's a practical possibility.

Five

Trials, Tribulations, and The Crucible

E very superhero, from the pages of comic books to the big screen, has to deal with challenges that expose their weaknesses. It's a universal theme in storytelling and a powerful metaphor for our lives. Superman faced Kryptonite, Spider-Man wrestled with responsibility, and Wonder Woman grappled with her commitment to justice. Why do these tales resonate with us so deeply? It's because no matter how strong, how powerful, how extraordinary we may feel, we are all prone to the same human experience, the difficulty of trials and tribulations.

Life is filled with challenges. There's no way around it, no shortcut through it. Trials and tribulations are not just part of our story; they're part of THE story, the human story, the epic tale of growth, development, overcoming.

Jesus' ministry was not a smooth, straightforward path; it was fraught with difficulty, opposition, and suffering. He was misunderstood by his family, falsely accused by the religious leaders, rejected by the very people He came to save. He endured storms, literal ones on the Sea of Galilee and metaphorical ones in the hearts and minds of those around Him. He faced temptations in the wilderness, was betrayed by one of His closest followers, and ultimately, suffered the unimaginable agony of the cross.

But here's where the story takes a profound turn. These trials, these challenges were not accidents; they were appointments. They were not random interruptions in the narrative; they were intentional invitations to something greater. Jesus's trials were not obstacles to His mission; they were opportunities for His purpose, windows into His true character, and a pathway to His destiny.

Just like our favorite superheroes, Jesus's weaknesses were exposed, not to defeat Him but to define Him, not to break Him but to build Him. They revealed His humanity, His compassion, His unwavering commitment to His mission. They unveiled a Savior who knew suffering, who understood pain, who felt abandonment, yet chose to press on, chose to endure, chose to triumph.

The story of Jesus's trials is a mirror to our own. It's a reminder that we too will face challenges, we too will experience pain, we too will grapple with our weaknesses. But it's also an encouragement, an inspiration, a call to see our trials not as enemies but as allies, not as hindrances but as helpers, not as stumbling blocks but as stepping stones.

The inevitable trials of life are not about what we endure; they're about who we become. They're not about our weaknesses; they're about our strength. They're not about our failures; they're about our faith. And like Jesus, like the superheroes we admire, we too can emerge from our trials not defeated but defined.

The inevitable trials await us all. The question is, will we face them with fear or with faith? Will we see them as obstacles or opportunities? Will we allow them to define us or will we use them to develop us?

Your tribulations are your triumph.

Trials and Purpose

How can trials focus us on our purpose? The idea might seem counterintuitive at first glance, but it becomes abundantly clear when we take a closer look at the nature of trials and the profound effect they can have on our lives.

It's because trials expose what's at the core of our being. They strip away the superficial, the distractions, the unessential, revealing what truly matters, what truly drives us, what truly defines us. They force us to face the hard questions, to grapple with the real issues, to confront the ultimate realities of our lives. Who are we really? What do we truly want? Where are we truly going?

These questions are not just philosophical musings; they are existential inquiries that get to the heart of our identity, our mission, our purpose.

Trials are like a refining fire, burning away the impurities, leaving only the pure, the genuine, the authentic. Just as gold is purified by intense heat, our character is purified by intense challenges. The impurities of doubt, fear, complacency are burned away, leaving behind the pure gold of faith, courage, commitment.

They sharpen our focus, heightening our awareness of what's truly important, what's truly at stake. They heighten our determination, galvanizing our will, energizing our effort. They deepen our faith, strengthening our trust, solidifying our belief. Trials don't just challenge us; they change us. They don't just test us; they teach us. They don't just confront us; they cultivate us.

They push us toward our destiny, pulling us into our calling. Just like the wind that pushes a ship toward its destination, trials push us toward ours. They pull us out of our comfort zone. They propel us forward, accelerating our progress, amplifying our potential.

Jesus knew this. He embraced His trials not as burdens but as bridges, bridges that connected His challenges to His calling. He saw them not as hindrances but as highways. He used them not as excuses but as experiences, experiences that shaped Him, strengthened Him, sustained Him, experiences that made Him who He was, who He is, who He will forever be.

The next time you find yourself in the heat of a trial, remember this: Your trial is not your enemy; it's your educator. Your struggle is not your setback; it's your stepping stone.

Sin and Shortcomings

In the rich tapestry of life, not all trials are thrust upon us by circumstance. Sometimes, the difficulties we face are the result of our own actions, our own choices, our own failures. This, in the Christian understanding, is what we call sin.

Sin is not merely a list of wrongdoings or a catalog of crimes. It's a condition, a state of being, a pervasive problem that affects all of us. In its simplest form, sin can be defined as "missing the mark" of how God created us to be.

God designed us for greatness, crafted us for completeness, destined us for wholeness. He wanted us to live fully empowered, wholly alive, beautifully blessed. Yet, we have a tendency to fall short of that glorious standard. We wander away from the path, lose sight of the purpose, drift from the destiny. That's what sin is all about.

But here's the good news: We don't have to remain in that state. We don't have to be trapped in our shortcomings, enslaved to our failures, chained to our mistakes.

Jesus: Our Redemption

Enter Jesus. He came not just to teach us or to inspire us, but to redeem us, to rescue us, to restore us.

He took our shortcomings upon Himself, bore our sins in His body, suffered our penalties on the cross. He took everything that hurt us, harmed us, hindered us, and nailed it to the cross. He made a way for us to be whole again, to be healed again, to be free again.

Remember the story of the ten lepers? They were outcasts, rejected, despised. But Jesus healed them. He touched them, transformed them, renewed them. But only one came back to thank Him. And the scripture said he was "sozo" (Luke 17:19). That Greek word means healed, set free, delivered. It's a comprehensive healing that touches every part of our being—body, soul, and spirit.

That's what God wants to do for each one of us. He wants to "sozo" us. He wants to heal our wounds, mend our brokenness, fill our emptiness. He wants to set us free from our chains, liberate us from our limits, release us from our restrictions. He wants to deliver us from our darkness, rescue us from our ruins, redeem us from our wreckage.

God wants to Sozo us from all that is trying to hurt us. He wants to restore us to the fullness of who we were created to be. He wants to help us hit the mark, reach the goal, fulfill the purpose.

But it requires something from us. It requires repentance, a turning away from our sinful ways, a coming back to God's path. It requires faith, a trust in Jesus, a reliance on His redemption. It requires gratitude, a thankfulness for His grace, an appreciation for His mercy.

The Way Forward

So, where does that leave us? It leaves us with a choice. A choice to remain in our sins or to embrace Jesus's salvation. A choice to continue in our shortcomings or to enter into God's wholeness. A choice to wallow in our weaknesses or to walk in God's strength.

The trials we create through sin don't have to be our undoing. They can be our awakening. They can be the very things that lead us back to God, back to wholeness, back to life.

The question is, will we come? Will we return? Will we be like the one leper who came back, grateful, healed, and whole?

Let's take the step. Let's embrace the healing. Let's live the life we were meant to live. Fully empowered. Completely whole. Sozo.

Six

Death and Rebirth

The death and resurrection of Jesus Christ is not just an event; it's the cornerstone of the Christian faith. It is the epitome of love, sacrifice, and victory. When Jesus breathed His last on that rugged cross, something extraordinary happened; it wasn't the tragic end of a compassionate teacher, but the decisive defeat of sin and death orchestrated by the Creator of the Universe.

In laying down His life, Jesus picked up all of our shortcomings—our guilt, our shame, our burdens—and nailed them to the cross. He looked into the face of our messy human condition and chose love, chose us. His resurrection is not merely a historical fact; it's an ongoing reality, offering new life, endless hope, and transformational power to all who believe in Him.

Imagine carrying a heavy backpack everywhere you go, day after day. That's what guilt feels like—a constant, crushing weight. It drains our energy, robs our joy, and skews our perspective, trapping us in a cycle of self-condemnation that's as exhausting as it is relentless. Guilt hunches us over spiritually, making it hard to look up and see the grace that is abundantly available to us.

Jesus understands this weight. He knows the agony of guilt, the way it can dominate our thoughts and darken our days. That's why He chose the cross—so that we might be free from this torment. When He declared, "It is finished," He was proclaiming the end of guilt's stronghold on our lives. He was announcing that our debts were paid, our slate wiped clean.

Now, imagine a life free from that weight, a life where the nagging lies of the enemy about your identity are silenced. Picture waking up every day knowing you are deeply loved, wholly accepted, and completely forgiven. Envision living unburdened, with a heart that's light and a spirit that's free to love, serve, and embrace the abundant life Jesus promises.

This isn't a fairy tale; it's the very reality that Jesus' death and resurrection secures for us. His sacrifice was the exchange of His perfect, sinless life for our broken, sinful ones. He took our guilt and shame to the grave and left them there, rising again to offer us a life defined not by our past, but by His love and righteousness.

Jesus doesn't just offer us an improved life; He offers us a new life, a rebirth. He invites us into a transformative relationship where we are no longer slaves to sin, but beloved children of God. We are given a new identity—one rooted in His love, not in the mistakes we've made or the lies we've believed.

Our Personal Cross: Shedding the Old Self

Just as Jesus died and was raised to life, we too are invited into a process of death and rebirth. This is not physical, but spiritual. It is the process of laying down our old self—the person we were before we knew Christ. The old attitudes, the old habits, the old ways of thinking that led us into sin and kept us from God's best for our lives. It's about surrendering who we were in order to embrace who we can be in Christ.

As Paul writes in 2 Corinthians 5:17, "Therefore, if anyone is in Christ, he is a new creation. The old has passed away; behold, the new has come." This isn't just a nice thought—it's a radical transformation.

It is important to understand that in this transformation, Jesus doesn't want to erase your personality or individuality. He created you uniquely, with purpose and intention, and He cherishes who you are. What Jesus aims to heal are the broken places in your heart, the fears that paralyze you, and the self-condemnation that keeps you in chains. He wants to lift the burdens that have been placed upon you—by the world, by other people, or by yourself.

Freedom, Not Confinement

Jesus' desire is to set you free, not pen you up. He is the Great Physician, skillfully tending to our wounds, mending what is broken, and nurturing us back to health. He doesn't look at us and see a project; He sees a beloved child. When He works within us, it is not to constrain us but to liberate us from the things that have held us captive. His aim is not to diminish our life but to allow us to fully live.

He wants to free you from the lies you've believed about your own worth. He wants to replace the voice of condemnation with words of love, to swap the chains of fear with the wings of faith. He invites you into freedom from the past, freedom from guilt, and freedom into a vibrant, love-filled future.

In Christ, you are invited to become your truest self—the person God envisioned when He created you. This is not a loss of self; it is the finding of self. It is coming home to who you were always meant to be: loved, free, and made whole in Christ. It is stepping into a life where your actions and decisions are no longer driven by fear or the need for approval but are the joyful response to God's boundless love for you.

So, as you stand at the threshold of this new life, remember that Jesus isn't asking you to become someone else. He's inviting you to become the person you were always destined to be—a child of God, radiant in His love, and alive in His freedom.

A Modern Parable: Neo's Journey in "The Matrix"

In the iconic science fiction film "The Matrix," we meet Neo, a hacker who discovers that the world he knows is actually a simulated reality. Neo is given a choice between a red pill, which would allow him to see the world as it truly is, and a blue pill, which would keep him in blissful ignorance. He chooses the red pill, effectively 'dying' to the world he knows.

As Neo takes the red pill, he is 'reborn' into the real world—a world vastly different from the one he has known. It is grim and harsh, but it is true and real. In this new world, Neo is not just another hacker; he is seen as the potential 'savior' of humanity, prophesied to break the chains of the Matrix and lead people into freedom.

Towards the end of the film, Neo is killed, mirroring a moment of death. But, in a climactic scene, he is revived—reborn—into a new state of being. In this moment, Neo rises, no longer constrained by the simulated rules of the Matrix. He sees everything for what it is and gains power he didn't have before. This mirrors the idea of resurrection, a passage from death into a new, empowered life, reminiscent of the Christian story of death and resurrection in Jesus.

The parallels here are profound. Just like Neo, we are offered a choice—to remain in the 'simulation' of our worldly lives or to wake up to a higher, truer reality in Christ. When we accept Christ, we are, in a sense, taking the 'red pill'. We die to our old selves, our old ways, and our old world. And just as Neo is reborn into a new reality with a vital mission and newfound abilities, we are reborn into a new life with Christ—empowered, free, and with a kingdom purpose.

"The Matrix" isn't a Christian movie, but Neo's journey—from ignorance to truth, from death to life, from bondage to freedom—is a powerful, modern-day parable of the spiritual journey that we are invited to take through Christ.

In Christ, we are called to die to our old selves—to our sin, our past, our mistakes, and our worldly ways. And in Him, we are reborn into something entirely new. Like Neo, we are not merely improved; we are transformed. We are not just better versions of ourselves; we are new creations.

The Empty Tomb: A Life Fully Lived

When Jesus rose from the dead, the tomb was empty. That empty tomb is emblematic of the life we're invited into—a life no longer defined by past mistakes, guilt, or shame. In Christ, we can step into a life fully lived, unrestricted by the constraints of our old selves.

The life Christ offers us is not a slightly improved version of our old life; it's a completely new, vibrant, purpose-filled existence. It's a life marked by love, joy, peace, and the fullness of God's Spirit. It's a life where anything is possible because we are no longer limited by our own strength, but are empowered by God's mighty power working within us.

Are there things you're carrying that you don't want to bear for the rest of your life? Lay them at the cross. At that cross, where Jesus was crucified, is where our old selves are crucified as well. And just as Jesus was raised, so we too are raised into a new way of life. We are reborn with Him—not physically, but spiritually. We become part of His resurrection story.

This is not just theology; it's transformation. It's not just doctrine; it's deliverance. It's not just history; it's our story. We are reborn, not into a slightly cleaner version of our old selves, but into a radically new life that reflects the character, the love, and the power of Christ Himself.

"I have been crucified with Christ. It is no longer I who live, but Christ who lives in me. And the life I now live in the flesh I live by faith in the Son of God, who loved me and gave himself for me." (Galatians 2:20)

Imagine a life free from the torment of guilt and the stain of past mistakes, because in Christ, there is forgiveness and the slate is wiped clean (1 John 1:9). Imagine living free from the constant weight of anxiety, because Jesus invites us to cast all our anxieties on Him (1 Peter 5:7).

Deliverance from Guilt and Shame: In Christ, our sins are not only forgiven, but forgotten. We are no longer defined by our past, but by His righteousness (2 Corinthians 5:21).

Deliverance from Fear and Anxiety: The resurrection power of Christ allows us to live with a peace that surpasses all understanding, guarding our hearts and minds in Christ Jesus (Philippians 4:7).

Deliverance from Bondage and Addiction: Whom the Son sets free is free indeed (John 8:36). Christ's resurrection breaks the chains that bind us.

Deliverance from Hopelessness and Despair: In Christ, we are filled with an everlasting hope, a future that is secure and bright (Jeremiah 29:11).

Deliverance from Loneliness and Isolation: In Christ, we are adopted into a loving family, the body of Christ, where we belong and are deeply known (Romans 8:15-16).

A New Life, A New Identity

This new life in Christ is not a mere self-improvement project; it's a complete transformation of our identity. We are not 'fixed' versions of our old selves; we are new creations, reborn in the likeness of Christ (Ephesians 4:24). We are not just patched up; we are brand new, with a new heart, a new spirit, and a new purpose that aligns with God's perfect and pleasing will for us (Romans 12:2).

This new birth is an invitation to live in the reality of God's love, grace, and power every day. It's about living out the truth that we are loved by God, accepted in Christ, and empowered by the Holy Spirit. Our old self, with all its sins and failures, is nailed to the cross, and the new self is alive, thriving in the love and power of Christ.

Death and rebirth—it's a journey that echoes the pattern of Christ Himself. In this transformative process, we find that our darkest moments can give birth to our brightest days, our deepest sorrows can lead to our most profound joys, and our most painful deaths can lead to our most glorious rebirths.

In Christ, we are invited into a narrative that is bigger than ourselves—a narrative that includes a cross, an empty tomb, and a life reborn in radiant resurrection power.

Seven

Transformation of Spirit

T he story of God's love for us is one that goes beyond mere words. It's an unfolding revelation that has the power to change our lives from the inside out. Let's dive into what makes this love so special, so transformative.

First, we must understand the nature of God's love. In the New Testament, the word "agape" is used to describe a love that is selfless, sacrificial, and unconditional. It's not a love that waits for us to earn it or prove ourselves worthy. It's a love that simply is, regardless of who we are or what we've done.

This is the love that God has for us. A love that doesn't measure, doesn't count, doesn't hold back.

God's acceptance is not something we work for; it's something we live in. As it says in Romans 5:8, "But God demonstrates His own love toward us, in that while we were still sinners, Christ died for us." He loved us before we ever loved Him. He accepted us while we were still far from Him.

Can you grasp the enormity of that? His love isn't dependent on our actions or our worthiness. Ephesians 2:8-9 reminds us, "For it is by grace you have been saved, through faith—and this is not from yourselves, it is the gift of God—not by works, so that no one can boast."

This perfect love doesn't just accept us; it transforms us. 1 John 4:18 tells us, "There is no fear in love. But perfect love drives out fear, because fear has to do with punishment. The one who fears is not made perfect in love."

God's love doesn't just change our standing with Him; it changes our very nature. It heals our fears, mends our brokenness, and fills us with a purpose that goes beyond ourselves.

Let us remember the unbreakable nature of God's love. As Romans 8:38-39 proclaims, "For I am convinced that neither death nor life, neither angels nor demons, neither the present nor the future, nor any powers, neither height nor depth, nor anything else in all creation, will be able to separate us from the love of God that is in Christ Jesus our Lord."

This love is not a fleeting emotion; it's an eternal bond. It's not a contract with terms and conditions; it's a covenant sealed by God Himself.

The revelation of God's love is not just a comforting thought; it's a life-altering truth. His acceptance is radical, His love is perfect, and His grace is beyond comprehension. In understanding His agape love, we find a pathway to transformation, a journey into a life marked by His presence, His purpose, and His peace.

Becoming an Agent of Change

In the beloved animated series "Avatar: The Last Airbender," Aang, the main protagonist, embodies the role of the Avatar—a unique figure who is the bridge between the human world and the spiritual realm. The Avatar's duty is to maintain balance and harmony among the four elements—Earth, Water, Air, and Fire—and the nations that represent them.

Aang's journey is filled with both challenges and triumphs as he grapples with his destiny and purpose. He discovers that being the Avatar is not just about mastering the bending of the elements; it's about leadership, wisdom, compassion, and a profound connection to the world around him. The Avatar is the one who can bring harmony to a world filled with chaos, division, and strife.

Now, think about a believer's journey in Christ. When we accept our calling and align ourselves with God's purpose, we become spiritual 'Avatars' in our own right. Just as Aang was chosen to restore balance to his world, we are chosen to bring a divine balance to ours.

The spiritual 'elements' in our lives—our emotions, our relationships, our purpose, our passions—all start to align with God's will as we submit to Him. It's a transformation that resonates within our very being and radiates outward.

Our actions, our words, and our love become conduits for God's grace and peace, touching the lives of those around us.

This transformation isn't always easy or straightforward. Much like Aang, we will face trials and struggles as we strive to live out our calling. Yet, the journey is worth it. As we grow in faith and obedience, we become more attuned to God's Spirit, allowing Him to work through us in ways that transcend human understanding.

We become agents of change, not through our power but through His. We bring harmony where there's discord, love where there's hatred, hope where there's despair. The impact goes far beyond our individual lives. It's about a cosmic alignment, a synchronization with God's eternal plan.

It's a call to spiritual harmony. It's a call to transformation. It's a call to be a living Avatar of God's love.

Fruits of the Spirit: A New Life

The life in Christ is not stagnant; it's dynamic, evolving, and ever-growing. As we abide in Him, the Holy Spirit begins to cultivate in us virtues that reflect the very nature of God. Love, joy, peace, patience, kindness, goodness, faithfulness, gentleness, and self-control—these are not just moral guidelines; they're the manifestation of the Divine in us. They're evidence of a life attuned to God's Spirit.

This transformation goes beyond mere behavior modification. It's a profound inner change that comes from being loved by God Himself. His perfect and selfless "agape" love inspires us to love others in the same way. We're not merely imitating Jesus; we're living in union with Him.

But the transformation doesn't end with our actions and attitudes; it also encompasses our thoughts and our mind. As Paul states in Romans 12:2, "Do not conform to the pattern of this world, but be transformed by the renewing of your mind." This renewing is the work of the Holy Spirit, aligning our thoughts with the thoughts of God, enabling us to "have the mind of Christ" (1 Corinthians 2:16).

The transformation of our minds is a radical shift in perspective. We start to see the world through God's eyes, understanding His heart and His desires. Our values, our priorities, our decision-making processes—all are reshaped by this divine perspective.

It's like a mental rebirth, where old thoughts, old prejudices, and old ways of thinking are replaced by the wisdom and insight that come from knowing God. We no longer think as the world thinks; we think as God thinks. We no longer live for ourselves; we live for Him.

This renewing of the mind is not a one-time event but a continual process. Every day, as we spend time in God's Word, as we pray, as we worship, we allow the Holy Spirit to reshape our thinking, to deepen our understanding, to refine our wisdom. It's a journey of discovery, where we learn to see ourselves, others, and the world as God sees them.

The Fruits of the Spirit are not just virtues we strive to attain; they're the natural outflow of a life surrendered to God. They're the visible signs of an invisible reality, the tangible evidence of a spiritual transformation that begins in the heart, extends to the mind, and manifests in every aspect of our lives.

In Christ, we don't just become better people; we become new people. We are reborn, not just in spirit but in mind, living as reflections of God's love, grace, and wisdom in a world that desperately needs to see Him.

Bringing Heaven to Earth: A Call to Action

The transformation doesn't stop with us. As God's love transforms us, we become agents of His grace in the world. We start reflecting His kingdom here on Earth, bringing healing, hope, justice, and compassion. We're called to be like leaven in dough, like light in darkness, bringing Heaven's touch to the Earth's weary places.

But this isn't merely a grand and abstract vision; it's a personal call to each one of us. Jesus spoke of this responsibility explicitly when he told us to love our neighbors as ourselves (Mark 12:31) and to treat the "least of these" with the same love and care as we would for Him (Matthew 25:40). Our neighbors, our community, those who are marginalized and struggling—they're not just people we pass by. They're our family in Christ, and how we treat them reflects our relationship with God.

This call to love and serve is not a burden but a privilege. It's a chance to live out our faith in tangible, meaningful ways. To feed the hungry, clothe the naked, visit the sick, welcome the stranger—these are not mere acts of charity; they're acts of worship, opportunities to show God's love in action.

It's a grand vision, and it's not without its challenges. But the same Spirit that empowered Jesus empowers us. We're not alone in this journey. God's Spirit guides us, mentors us, and helps us—turning us into living Avatars of His grace, aligning our world with His divine love and purpose.

This transformation is not a fantasy; it's a reality for anyone who chooses to walk with God. It's about taking responsibility for the world around us, recognizing that our faith has hands and feet, that it moves and acts, that it cares and loves.

The question is, are you ready to take your place as God's chosen instrument of transformation? The journey is incredible, and the impact is eternal. It's about more than personal growth; it's about global change. It's about bringing Heaven's love, justice, and mercy to Earth, one act of kindness at a time.

It's about following Jesus's example and embracing His call to be light in the darkness, salt in the decay, hope in the despair. It's about living a life that matters, a life that resonates with God's heart, a life that brings Heaven to Earth.

And it all starts with a simple yet profound decision—to love God, to love others, and to let that love shape everything we do.

Eight

Atonement, Healing, and Reconciliation

L et's be honest: forgiveness isn't easy. We've all been hurt, betrayed, let down. Maybe it's a family member who let us down at the worst possible time. Perhaps it's a coworker who took credit for your hard work. Or it could be something deeper, more painful that's been a burden for years.

Here's where it gets interesting. At the core of our faith is something that seems almost too good to be true. Because of what Jesus did for us, we're not only forgiven; we're invited into a lifestyle of forgiveness.

I know, I know, it sounds difficult. Almost unnatural. But stick with me.

Why Forgiveness?

See, forgiveness isn't just a nice idea; it's a command from Jesus Himself. He taught us to forgive others as we've been forgiven. He didn't say it would be easy, but He did say it would be freeing.

Think about what Jesus endured. Take a moment and really consider it. The betrayal by one of His closest friends. The denial by Peter, who swore he would never leave Him. The injustice of His trial, where lies and politics led to a brutal execution. It's overwhelming, isn't it?

Yet, His words on the cross were, "Father, forgive them, for they do not know what they are doing" (Luke 23:34). Just imagine that. He's in pain, He's suffering, He's dying—and He's praying for the very people who put Him there. If anyone had a right to hold a grudge, it was Him. But He chose forgiveness.

And here's something even more mind-boggling: Jesus didn't just forgive those who wronged Him that day. His forgiveness reaches beyond that hill, beyond that moment in time. It stretches out to all of us. That's a lot of forgiveness. Because when Jesus died on that cross, He died for all sins—for your sins, for my sins, for the sins of the entire world. For all time. Everywhere.

Now, let's break that down because it's too big to take in all at once.

It's Personal: Jesus died for you. He knows every mistake you've ever made, every thoughtless word, every selfish act. And He says, "I forgive you."

It's Universal: Jesus' death wasn't just for the believers, or the good people, or the ones who try really hard. It was for everyone. That means your neighbor, your coworker, your worst enemy. All forgiven.

It's Eternal: This isn't a one-time offer that's going to expire. Jesus' forgiveness is as true today as it was 2,000 years ago, and it will be just as true tomorrow.

So what does that mean for us? Well, if we're following Jesus —if we're trying to live like Him—then we have to follow His example. And that means forgiving. Not just the small slights and daily annoyances, but the deep, painful wounds. The ones that seem impossible to heal.

But remember, with Jesus, nothing is impossible. He's already done the heavy lifting. He's shown us the way. All we have to do is walk in His footsteps.

And I know, it's hard. But when we consider what He's done for us—when we realize the magnitude of His love and forgiveness—how can we do anything less?

Now here's the invitation for you and me: to walk in His footsteps. To live a life marked not by bitterness but by grace. To free ourselves from the chains of unforgiveness that keep us bound to the past.

Can you imagine what that looks like? It's relationships restored. It's the weight lifted off your shoulders. It's the peace that comes from letting go of that old grudge. It's living with a clear conscience, knowing that you've done what's right, even when it's hard.

I won't sugarcoat it. It's not an overnight transformation. It's a journey, a process. But it's also an incredible opportunity to experience God's grace in a way that not only changes us but can change those around us.

If we really believe that we're forgiven, completely and utterly forgiven, how can we not extend that same forgiveness to others?

Letting Go of Others' Wrongs

You know that person who wronged you? The one whose memory makes your blood boil? I think we've all got someone like that in our lives. And it's tough, isn't it? The pain, the anger, the resentment—it can all feel like a burden too heavy to bear.

But here's what Jesus says about that. He says, "Let it go." And I know, that sounds too simple, too easy. But it's not about letting them off the hook. It's about setting yourself free. It's like taking a splinter out of your soul. You don't have to carry that pain anymore.

Remember when Peter asked Jesus how often he should forgive someone? He thought seven times was pretty generous. But Jesus said, "I tell you, not just seven times, but seventy-seven times" (Matthew 18:22). And He wasn't just talking about numbers. He was talking about a way of life.

So how do we get there? How do we take this radical idea and turn it into reality? Here are some practical steps:

Recognize the Need for Forgiveness: It starts with acknowledging the hurt. You can't forgive something you won't admit.

Choose to Forgive: It's a decision. Not a feeling. Decide to let go of the desire for revenge, the need to be right. It's hard, but it's worth it.

Seek God's Help: Pray about it. Ask God to give you the strength to forgive. Lean into His love and grace.

Extend Empathy: Try to see things from their perspective. It doesn't excuse what they did, but it can help you understand.

Rebuild if Possible: If it's safe and appropriate, consider rebuilding the relationship. But remember, forgiveness doesn't always mean reconciliation, especially if there is abuse or violence involved.

Repeat as Needed: Forgiveness is a process, not a one-time event. It might take 77 times 7 in a day. That's okay. Keep going.

I know it's tough. Believe me, I've been there. But forgiveness isn't just a nice idea. It's a command from our Savior. It's a path to freedom, to healing, to a life unburdened by bitterness.

And here's the best part: You don't have to do it alone. The same Jesus who commands us to forgive also promises to walk with us every step of the way. He knows what it's like to be wronged, and He's ready to guide us through it.

Bigger than Personal Grudges

But wait, it gets bigger. It's not just about individuals; it's about systems, institutions. We live in a broken world, and yes, it fails us. Sometimes, it fails us in ways that are almost impossible to comprehend. But holding onto anger? It won't fix anything. Forgiveness can be the first step towards change.

You might be sitting there, thinking, "David, you don't know what I've been through. You don't know what the church, what these institutions have done to me." And you're right; I don't know your story. But I know this: bitterness won't heal your pain. Anger won't make things right.

Now, let's be clear about something: Forgiving institutions that have hurt you by their negligence is more about releasing yourself from bitterness. You're doing it for your heart, not to release them from accountability. There needs to be justice. There needs to be accountability. But there also needs to be forgiveness.

Let's dig into this a little more:

The Reality of Institutional Hurt: Sometimes, the very places meant to heal us wound us instead. The church, which is supposed to be a place of love and compassion, can end up hurting people on a deep level. Maybe that's part of your story. And if it is, I'm so sorry. The pain is real, and it's profound.

The Necessity of Healing: While you carry around trauma, which has to be healed in time, what you can't carry around is bitterness, anger, and hatred. It's like a poison, eating you up from the inside. It won't change what happened, but it will change you. And not for the better.

The Power of Forgiveness: Forgiveness isn't about saying, "It's okay." It's not about excusing or minimizing. It's about letting go of the hold that bitterness has on your soul. It's about choosing a better way, even when it feels impossible.

The Pursuit of Justice: Forgiveness doesn't mean we ignore injustice. It doesn't mean we let people off the hook. It means we approach the pursuit of justice with a heart free from hatred. It means we seek what's right without being consumed by what's wrong.

Jesus knew all about injustice. He knew all about betrayal. And yet, His response was forgiveness. Not because it was easy, but because it was right. And because it set Him free to love, to heal, to change the world.

So maybe today, it's time to take a step. Maybe it's time to choose forgiveness, even when it feels impossible. Maybe it's time to let go of the bitterness and pick up the hope, the healing, the love that Jesus offers.

Because here's the truth: The world needs justice. But it also needs grace. It needs accountability. But it also needs forgiveness. And as followers of Jesus, we're called to walk in both. Not because it's easy, but because it's the way of the one who forgave us first.

Stop Beating Yourself Up

Now, here's a tricky one: forgiving ourselves. We all mess up. We all have regrets. We all have those moments we wish we could take back. But living in guilt? That's not God's plan for you. He's already forgiven you. Maybe it's time you did the same.

Let's break it down and take a look at what this means for your life:

Recognize Your Humanity: First and foremost, let's just be honest. You're human, and humans make mistakes. We all have those cringe-worthy memories that make us want to hide our face in our hands. The embarrassing moments, the poor decisions, the "what was I thinking?" experiences. That's part of being human. It's how we learn and grow.

Forgive Your Younger Self: Now, this is where it gets personal. Think back to those mistakes, those stupid things you've done. Can you forgive your younger self for those? There's no shame in being naive. There's no shame in learning the hard way. Love your inner child. Embrace the growth that came from those experiences. Your past mistakes have shaped you, but they don't define you.

Embrace God's Forgiveness: Sometimes, the hardest person to forgive is ourselves. But here's the incredible truth: God has already forgiven you. The Creator of the universe looks at you, with all your flaws and failures, and says, "You are loved. You are forgiven." If God can forgive you, don't you think it's time to forgive yourself?

Move Forward with Grace: Forgiving yourself isn't about erasing the past; it's about embracing the future. It's about moving forward without the heavy baggage of guilt and shame. It's about walking in the freedom and joy that God intends for you. And guess what? That's not just possible; it's what you were created for.

Extend That Grace to Others: One of the beautiful things about forgiving yourself is that it frees you to extend that same grace to others. When you understand your own need for forgiveness, it becomes a lot easier to forgive the people around you. And in a world that's often harsh and judgmental, that's a breath of fresh air.

Here's the bottom line: You don't have to live in guilt and shame. You don't have to be held back by the mistakes of your past. God has a better way for you. And it starts with embracing His forgiveness and extending that forgiveness to yourself.

You might be thinking, "David, that's easier said than done." And you're right. Forgiveness, especially self-forgiveness, is a journey. It takes time. It takes effort. It takes grace. But it's a journey worth taking.

So today, why not take a step? Why not look in the mirror and say to yourself, "I forgive you. I love you. And I'm excited about the future God has for you." It might feel a little awkward at first. It might feel a little scary. But it might also be the start of something beautiful. It might be the start of the life God has always intended for you.

"Everything, Everywhere, All at Once"

Have you ever felt caught in a whirlwind of choices, relationships, and dreams, unsure which path to take? Well, there's a movie out there, "Everything Everywhere All at Once," that paints a fascinating picture of what that can look like. It's a story that resonates with something deep inside all of us, something that echoes with the very fabric of our faith.

Picture this: Evelyn, a middle-aged woman, discovers that she can jump between parallel universes. Cool, right? But it's more than just a sci-fi adventure. This ability takes her on a journey across countless choices and what-ifs. It's a lot like life, isn't it? You make a choice, and suddenly, you're down a path you never expected.

Now, here's where it gets really interesting. Evelyn learns to fight not with weapons but with empathy, love, and kindness. Sound familiar? It should, because that's exactly what Jesus calls us to do. Remember Romans 8:38-39? Nothing can separate us from the love of Christ. Not death, not life, not even jumping between universes!

What struck me about this film is how it mirrors our own journey with Christ. Evelyn's struggle to accept and forgive her daughter, her desire to be a better version of herself, her realization that love is what truly matters—all of these themes are at the core of our faith.

And you know what else? Evelyn's journey isn't just about self-discovery. It's about community, relationships, and reconciliation. It's a story that goes beyond the individual and affects everyone around her. Kind of like the love of Christ, don't you think?

So, what can we learn from this incredible story? First, that our choices matter, and they resonate in ways we may never fully grasp. Second, that forgiveness, love, and empathy are powerful forces that can change our world. And most importantly, that God's love for us is so profound, so radical, that it transforms us into something new.

Maybe, just maybe, this movie is a reminder that we're all part of something bigger. That we're all connected. That we're all loved by a God who sees us as we truly are and loves us anyway. And that, my friends, is a love worth embracing.

Creating a Community Like No Other

Imagine a community where forgiveness flows like water. Where people are free from judgment, free from resentment, free to love and be loved. That's not a fantasy; it's the church Jesus envisioned. It's what happens when we live in forgiveness.

And it's not just Jesus. The Apostle Paul caught this vision too. He spent letter after letter writing to the first-century churches, imploring them to live in peace with one another. He knew that forgiveness wasn't just a personal thing; it was a community thing. It was the heart and soul of the church.

Consider what Paul wrote in Colossians 3:13: "Bear with each other and forgive one another if any of you has a grievance against someone. Forgive as the Lord forgave you."

He's saying, "Hey, we're all in this together. We all make mistakes. Let's give each other the grace that God has given us."

Or what about Ephesians 4:32? "Be kind and compassionate to one another, forgiving each other, just as in Christ God forgave you."

Again, the message is clear: Forgiveness is not optional. It's essential. It's the glue that holds the community of believers together.

Now, let's get practical. What does this look like for us today?

Embracing Grace: It starts with embracing the grace that God has given us. When we realize how much we've been forgiven, it becomes a lot easier to extend that forgiveness to others.

Letting Go of the Little Things: Sometimes, the biggest obstacles to community are the little annoyances, the petty grievances. Can we let those go? Can we choose peace over perfection?

Facing the Big Hurts: And yes, sometimes, there are big hurts. Deep wounds. Those take time and effort to heal. But the journey towards forgiveness is always worth it.

Forgiving Systems and Institutions: And as we talked about earlier, it's not just about forgiving individuals. It's about forgiving the systems and institutions that fail us. That's harder, no doubt. But it's a part of the journey.

Building Community: Finally, it's about building that community. It's about creating a space where everyone is welcome, where everyone is loved, where everyone is free to be who God created them to be.

That's the church Jesus envisioned. That's the church Paul worked so hard to build. And that's the church we're called to be a part of.

Who's with me? Because let me tell you, when we do this, we're not just following a set of religious rules. We're joining a movement that has the power to change hearts, to change lives, to change the world.

Nine

Everyday Adventure

S o, here we are. The hero's journey is almost complete. We've faced the trials, we've fought the battles, we've tasted victory. Just like in Star Wars, we've blown up the Death Star and saved the universe. Remember that scene?

Picture it: The Death Star, a massive, looming sphere of menace, armed with the power to obliterate entire planets. The Rebel Alliance, a ragtag band of heroes, going up against impossible odds. The tension is palpable as X-wing fighters zip through the narrow trenches of the Death Star, pursued by Imperial TIE fighters, lasers flashing in the black void of space.

And then, the moment of triumph. The crucial torpedo shot, guided by the Force, finds its mark. The Death Star erupts into a brilliant explosion, a triumph not just of firepower but of faith, courage, and persistence.

The galaxy is saved. The oppressive Empire is defeated. The heroes return, their faces glowing with the joy of victory. Medals are bestowed. The music swells. The crowd cheers. But in the midst of the celebration, there's a lingering question, an unspoken curiosity that tugs at the soul.

What now? What comes after this amazing death, rebirth, and revelation?

That's a question not just for a fictional galaxy far, far away. It's a question for us, here and now, on our own hero's journey with Jesus. We've tasted victory. We've seen God's power at work. We've been given our medals, so to speak.

But what's next? What does God have in store for us once the confetti has settled, and the parade has ended?

Well, my friends, that's where the real adventure begins. That's where we step into the everyday glory of walking with Jesus, of living a life filled with purpose, joy, and endless possibility.

The Death Star is destroyed. The enemy is defeated. But the journey? It's far from over. In fact, it's just beginning.

Buckle up, because the adventure ahead is unlike anything you've ever imagined.

Living in Victory

You see, with Jesus in our lives, every day becomes an adventure beyond our wildest dreams. It's not just a matter of going through the motions, clocking in and out of a mundane existence. It's about embracing a journey filled with excitement, hope, and meaning.

We are loved, filled, whole, and headed for our destiny. God's love isn't a fleeting emotion; it's a steadfast, unbreakable bond. It's a love that defines us, fuels us, and sends us forth with a purpose.

And heaven? It's right around the corner. Forget those old images of a stingy, cloud-and-harp heaven, where all we do is float aimlessly in some ethereal space. Heaven is vibrant, alive, full of adventure and excitement. It's a place of joy, connection, creativity, and endless exploration.

But we're not there yet. So how do we remain on earth? How do we live in this everyday victory?

We return to others who are in need of that same adventure in their lives. We don't keep this joy to ourselves; we share it. We reach out. We love. We serve.

We walk side by side with Jesus, who leads us onward into battles and victories. Not the battles of anger, revenge, or petty disputes, but battles of compassion, justice, and grace. We fight not for ourselves, but for others. We fight for those who are marginalized, oppressed, and forgotten.

Because Jesus rose from the grave, we don't fight to gain victory. We fight from a place of victory. The war is won. The grave is empty. Death has been defeated. We have the keys to death, hell, and the grave.

We have seen the end of the story – and we win.

But winning isn't the end; it's the beginning. It's the starting point for a life of continual growth, discovery, and joy. It's an invitation to live each day with courage, knowing that we are more than conquerors through Christ.

So take up the challenge. Embrace the adventure. Don't settle for a life of mediocrity when you were made for greatness. Live in the victory of Jesus, and watch how it transforms not only your life but the world around you.

"For everyone born of God overcomes the world. This is the victory that has overcome the world, even our faith" (1 John 5:4).

Now, here are some practical steps for continuing this victorious journey with Jesus:

Stay Connected with God

We've got to stay connected with God through prayer, reading the Bible, and seeking His guidance. "Pray without ceasing," as 1 Thessalonians 5:17 tells us. Our relationship with God is the fuel for our adventure. This is where our strength comes from, where our purpose is found. It's not just a once-a-week connection; it's a daily, hourly, moment-by-moment reliance on Him. If we neglect this, our spiritual life starts to run on empty.

Serve Others

Remember, it's not all about us. We're called to be the hands and feet of Jesus, serving those in need. "For even the Son of Man did not come to be served, but to serve," says Mark 10:45. This means reaching out, getting involved, helping, and loving others. It's about living selflessly and recognizing the needs of those around us. It's not a burden; it's a privilege, and it's an opportunity to show God's love in tangible ways.

Embrace Community

We need each other. We need friends, family, fellow believers to walk this journey with us. The early Christians "devoted themselves to the apostles' teaching and to fellowship" (Acts 2:42). We should do the same. We should find a church, a small group, or some friends who can encourage, challenge, and support us. Community helps us grow, keeps us accountable, and provides us with the love and companionship we were designed to crave.

Celebrate the Wins

Don't forget to celebrate the victories, big and small. Rejoice in what God is doing in your life and the lives of those around you. "Rejoice in the Lord always. I will say it again: Rejoice!" (Philippians 4:4). Sometimes we're so focused on the next goal that we forget to pause and give thanks. We should regularly take time to reflect, appreciate, and celebrate what God has done. It builds our faith and gives us a joyful heart.

Keep Moving Forward

The adventure never ends. There's always more to learn, more to do, more to become. Like Paul says in Philippians 3:14, "I press on toward the goal to win the prize for which God has called me heavenward in Christ Jesus." The Christian life isn't stagnant; it's dynamic, growing, evolving. We shouldn't become complacent or satisfied with the status quo. God has so much more in store for us if we're willing to press on.

Remember Who You Are

As a final note, never lose sight of your identity in Christ. You are a beloved child of God, saved, redeemed, and set free. "See what great love the Father has lavished on us, that we should be called children of God!" (1 John 3:1). That's who you are. That's your value. That's your purpose. Let that truth guide every decision, every relationship, every adventure.

These practical steps aren't just a formula; they're a lifestyle. They're the habits that help us live fully and faithfully in Christ. They're the means by which we grow, love, and make a difference in this world.

So take them to heart. Put them into practice. Live them out every day, and watch how God uses you to change the world around you. The adventure awaits, and the victory is yours.

Now go live it!So, are you ready? Are you ready to live this adventure every single day?

Because here's the thing: The victory is already won. The keys are in our hands. We know how the story ends.

All we have to do is live it. All we have to do is step out in faith, follow Jesus, and embrace the everyday adventure that awaits.

Let's make the most of it. Let's live the victory.

Who's with me?

Epilogue

Now it is your journey. You fill the pages in the Book of Life with what you do with this amazing gift of God's love and His promise to always be there for you. To strengthen and guide you. There's no set path, no predetermined outcome. It's an open adventure, one that's uniquely yours.

The story we've walked through together is not confined to the pages of this book. It's alive; it's moving; it's waiting for you to step in and take your place. You're not just a passive reader; you're an active participant. You're the hero.

If you need further encouragement, if you need friends and fellow adventurers, you can log on to SowEpic.com and find a community that shares your interests, that will love and accept you. You're not alone. There are others on this journey, and they're eager to walk with you.

My prayer for you is that you will become the hero in your story and live the amazing life you were meant to. I pray that you'll embrace the adventure, overcome the obstacles, celebrate the victories, and grow ever closer to the God who loves you so.

The journey is never really complete. You will walk through this cycle at momentous times in your life. When you need it, place this book where you can find it, and we will take this journey again together. The story doesn't end; it just takes new turns, opens new chapters, and offers new opportunities.

With this, dear reader, I invite you to step into your story, to take up the mantle, to become the hero you were meant to be. The pages are waiting to be filled. The adventure is calling. And I'm here, cheering you on, praying for you, and believing in the incredible things God will do in and through you.

May your journey be filled with wonder, joy, and purpose. May you find the strength, courage, and faith to face whatever comes your way. And may you always know that you're not alone, that God is with you, and that the best is yet to come.

Keep the faith. Keep moving forward. Keep living the adventure.

-David Lee

Made in the USA
Columbia, SC
20 January 2024

30728248R10046